Contents

Foreword

Many of you who have small brothers or sisters will want to help with their care. This book has been written to help you learn how to give that help.

Previous editions, under the title of "Junior Mothercraft Manual" and written by Dr. Susan M. Tracy and Dr. A. P. Norman, have been excellent guides for many Junior Red Cross members over past years, and now we are delighted to have this up-to-date version with a new title, written for us by Dr. David Harvey, MB, BS, MRCP, MRCS, D.Obst, RCOG, Consultant Paediatrician at Queen Charlotte's Hospital.

It is also a pleasure to acknowledge the help we have received from the Royal College of Nursing and National Council of Nurses, the Royal College of Midwives, the Queen's Institute of District Nursing and our own Branch Nursing Officers who have given invaluable advice and guidance in the production of this Manual.

A clear and interesting book can make learning easy and enjoyable. We are sure this one will help you to acquire the skills of looking after a baby and helping its mother.

Those of you who intend to be doctors, hospital or nursery nurses will find it especially interesting and we are most grateful to our three doctor friends for sharing with us their expert knowledge and professional experience.

Muriel Skeet

CHIEF NURSING OFFICER
British Red Cross Society

The expectant mother

When a baby is born, he is almost helpless and has to depend on his parents for all the things he needs. If left to himself he will die and he therefore needs protection and care until he is able to look after himself. The baby needs love as much as physical things, so that a baby born into a loving contented family has an excellent start in life. Everybody in a family has a part to play, the mother, the father, sons and daughters. Nowadays, it is much more useful for work in the home to be shared between husband and wife. Many fathers enjoy helping their wives by feeding the baby and changing nappies—showing that it is now old fashioned to think of child care as "woman's work".

Pregnancy

This is a period of nine months during which mothers carry their unborn babies in their bodies. The baby is inside the womb, or uterus, and is surrounded by a sac of fluid. The umbilical cord is attached to the baby's navel and to the placenta, or afterbirth, on the inside wall of the uterus. This cord contains blood vessels and the baby is nourished by his mother's blood stream as her blood flows through the placenta. As the nine months go by, the mother's abdomen gets much larger to accommodate the growing baby. Her body also prepares itself to nourish the baby after birth—her breasts get larger as they prepare to produce the milk which the baby will need when he has been born.

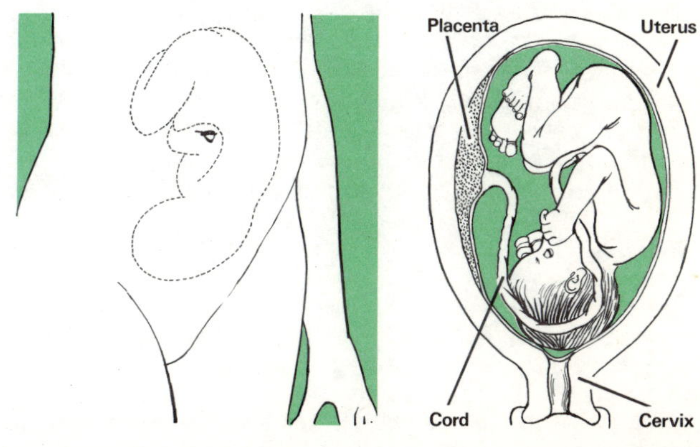

If a pregnant woman is to have healthy children, she must look after her own health. It is very important for her to have regular medical care so that any illnesses which might affect her, or the baby, can be detected. All minor ailments, such as bad teeth, should be put right and it is important for her to eat well. Her husband and her children should help her with her housework, because as the baby grows larger she will be less active and will get tired more easily.

A baby is born without teeth, but they are growing in the gums while the baby is growing in his mother's womb. It is therefore essential that the diet of the pregnant woman should include enough vitamin D and calcium, as these are responsible for good bone development. A woman can ensure that she is taking enough by drinking plenty of milk and can also take vitamin supplements if the doctor advises this.

A pregnant woman should lead an active life, with a reasonable amount of exercise. Although it is important that she should rest whenever she feels tired or if the doctors think it is necessary, there is no need for her to lead a sheltered, protected life. Many women continue working until one or two months before the baby is due.

Labour

At the end of nine months the baby is born by the process known as labour. The uterus is a muscular sac, which begins to contract and pushes the baby into the outside world through the birth canal or vagina. Most births in Great Britain today take place in hospital, because it is believed that this is safer for both the mother and baby. However, some mothers who are not expected to have any difficulty in labour, can safely be delivered by a midwife at home. This is ideal for the mother and her family as it means that the new baby can be looked after by the family at once and the mother is not separated from her other children. Nowadays, many hospitals arrange for the mother to go home one or two days after she has been delivered.

The baby is usually born head first through the vagina and as soon as he has been born the midwife or doctor attending the mother will tie the umbilical cord. Soon after the birth of the baby, the mother passes the placenta and cord. The baby does not need them any longer because after birth he obtains the oxygen he needs by breathing and the food he needs by mouth. The placenta and cord must not be thrown away until the doctor has looked at them.

During the first few days after birth the baby will gradually take more and more food and his body adapts itself to the outside world. The parents will often have many questions about the feeding and care of the new baby and those concerned with child welfare aim to help mothers and fathers, boys and girls, to look after babies and give them the best chance of growing up strong and healthy.

Improvements in Child Health

There have been great improvements in child health during this century. 70 years ago, 150 out of every 1,000 babies born died before the age of 1 year. Today, less than 20 babies die during the first year of life. The infant mortality rate, (i.e. the number of infant deaths per 1,000 live births), is therefore about one seventh of what it was 70 years ago.

Many advances have contributed to this improvement such as changes in education, new housing, and higher standards of living. Parents' expectations of health services for their children have increased, and child health services have expanded. Infant Welfare Centres of the past have been followed by Child Health Centres. Parents are encouraged to bring their babies and young children to these centres for assessment of their child's progress and air any queries they may have. Some family doctors arrange special sessions for mothers with babies and young children; these sessions are arranged at their own surgeries or at the health centre, at a time when sick people are not attending, so that the dangers of babies picking up infections are avoided.

Doctors and nurses who are specially trained in the care of children attend the Child Health Centre. Health visitors are trained nurses, who have undertaken further study and experience in family health. They visit families with young children, paying an initial visit when the mother comes home from hospital, or is transferred from the care of the midwife. The health visitor is always available if parents have health worries. A timely word may be all that is required, but if a seemingly minor problem needs more expert advice this can be referred early to the appropriate doctor or social worker. The health visitor works very closely with the family doctor, with the paediatrician who is a specialist in children's medicine, and with all other medical, nursing and social work personnel.

All these people are concerned with the promotion of health. Early detection of defects, such as a baby's inability to see or hear properly, means that help can be given and the effect of this disability on other aspects of development lessened.

While the majority of children are healthy, the child health service is directed towards keeping them so during the years when growth and development are proceeding most rapidly.

Mothers can receive advice about preparing for their newborn babies and the ways of feeding them. They are told what foods are essential or valuable, how to clothe the baby so that he is warm, but not too hot. They need to know how certain foods can protect babies from infection and disease and how by vaccination and immunization we can prevent illnesses such as smallpox, diptheria, whooping cough, tetanus, and poliomyelitis—diseases that can cause paralysis or death.

Many mothers have worries about growing babies and it often helps them to discuss these problems with the doctor or nurse at the Child Health Centre. They will need to know more about keeping children happy and preventing those fears, worries and troubles which, although they may not seem important to adults, are very serious to young children. Children need, above all, the love of their parents and the security of a happy home.

Preparing for baby

If possible, the room chosen for the baby should be light and airy and, ideally, have a window facing south so that it gets the maximum amount of sunlight. If the room is upstairs it is important to have a gate at the top of the staircase and precautions should be taken to prevent children falling from windows. Bars can be put across the window and the safety catch will prevent the window being opened too far.

Heating

The newborn baby can very easily get cold and his room will need to be adequately heated, especially in winter. A suitable temperature for the newborn baby's room is about 21 °C (70 °F). Central heating or oil-filled electric radiators are probably the safest form of heating, but unfortunately are not always available. If open fires (burning coal or a smokeless fuel), gas or electric fires or paraffin oil stoves are used then the source of heat must be carefully protected by a fire guard. This should be firmly fastened to the wall to cover the top of the fire so that later the baby cannot throw things into the fire or climb over the guard. An oil heater must stand out of the draught and where it cannot be knocked over; it should never be left burning all night and should be used with great care as many deaths are caused by fires from oil heaters.

Gas and electric fires should have taps or switches that are out of the baby's reach and not on the floor where he can play with them and accidentally turn them on. Accidents are dealt with in a later chapter.

Ventilation and Lighting

It is important that the room should be ventilated, but this must be achieved without draughts. It is usual to ventilate a room by leaving the window open and in this case it may be necessary to have a screen round the cot. It is always important to check the temperature in the baby's room and to remember that if a window is left open during the night in winter the room could become very cold which could be dangerous to a new-born baby. However, if there is not enough fresh air circulating in the room the air will soon become stale. Although stale air is not dangerous to the baby the room will be stuffy and uncomfortable for him.

The window should be large enough to allow sunlight to enter the room. Sunlight helps the baby to create Vitamin D in his own body which will prevent him from developing rickets. A night light may be necessary in the room; some children need a light in the room and others are quite happy to sleep in the dark.

Decoration

Light colours will help to make the room look larger and brighter. High gloss washable paint and vinyl papers are easily cleaned of grubby, sticky finger marks and it is a good idea to have a formica area or a blackboard on a lower part of one of the walls so that at a later stage the child can write or draw as he wishes. If the house is old, all old paint must be carefully stripped off as some of it may be lead paint and this is very dangerous to a small child if he eats it.

The floor should be completely covered with some material which is easy to clean and warm to kneel on. A wooden floor can be dangerous because of the splinters which the baby may get when he starts to crawl. If rugs are used it is important to make sure that they are of a non-slip type.

Curtains should be of some washable and non-inflammable material and there are many attractive patterns available.

Furniture

When the baby begins to crawl he will need all the available floor space to play on, so there should be as little furniture as possible in his room. However, certain items are essential.

The Cot Many parents find a carry cot very useful indeed when the baby is small. The baby can sleep comfortably in it; it can be carried from one room to the other. Carry cots are made in waterproof fabric and are therefore easily cleaned; they can be put onto a frame to become a pram and they are also useful if the baby is to be taken out in a car as the cot will lie on the back seat and the baby need not be disturbed. If a carry cot is to be used in a car, it is important that special straps are bought which will keep the cot on the seat of the car if there is an accident. After the first few weeks a larger cot will be required, about 120cm. (4 feet) long; a drop-sided wooden cot is probably the most hardwearing. The cot bars should not be more than 7 cm. (about 3 inches) apart, otherwise the baby may put his head between them and get it stuck.

Bedding The cot will need a firm mattress which, preferably, should be encased in a waterproof material as this will mean it can be easily cleaned when soiled. An under-blanket should cover the mattress and the baby can sleep between two flannelette or cotton sheets and covered by two blankets. A counterpane or eiderdown can be put on top of this. These days, many parents prefer to let the baby sleep in a sleeping bag which is comfortable and very warm.

Remember that a baby's bed clothes must be warm but light. He should never be so hot that his head becomes damp with sweat. A pillow is not necessary and is dangerous.

Bath Most baby baths are made of plastic. They can be bought to fit on to a stand, which can sometimes be used for the carry cot. Other baths can fit over an adult bath.

Trolley, Table or Working Surface This will be needed for bathing or changing the baby.

Cupboards A small wardrobe or a chest of drawers will be needed for the baby's clothes. A toy cupboard with low shelves that a child can reach will also be needed. Any cupboards must be firmly built or fixed to the wall so that a young child cannot pull the whole cupboard over on top of him.

Play Pen A play pen is very useful when the baby has started to crawl and when he wishes to pull himself on to his feet and try to walk. It should be placed on a rug on the floor with plenty of toys. Although he can be safely left alone in the play pen for a short while, while his mother is cleaning the next room for example, he should not be kept in it for any length of time, for a baby can feel restricted and even "caged" in such a small space.

Chairs The mother will need a low chair when she is feeding or dressing the baby. When the baby is older he will also need a chair with a tray which can be used for meals. It is safer to buy a low chair than a high one which may be unsteady and can fall over.

Toys

The small baby will only need simple things such as rattles and teething rings, but one must remember to wash the toys frequently. Toys which he will need when he is older are described in a later chapter.

If the baby's room is shared with older brothers and sisters, each child should, if possible, have his own drawer or small cupboard where he can put away his own things.

The baby's clothes

It is now possible to buy many simple practical garments for babies. One must remember that clothing is to keep the baby warm without allowing him to become too hot or restricting his movements. The baby should be dressed according to the weather and not the time of year—he may need a warm coat on a cold day even if it is mid-summer.

Babies' clothes today are often made of a mixture of materials. Synthetic fibres are very popular because they are easily washable and they can be mixed with other materials, such as cotton, to make very practical and warm garments. Wool is much less used today, but many babies will have small garments knitted for them by close relatives and friends. The baby will soon grow out of these clothes and more practical things can then be bought for him.

The clothes a baby will need will include vests, night gowns or dresses which can be used for both day or night wear, matinée jackets which must be made of something easily washable as they get soiled very frequently, and a shawl or wrap. A flannelette sheet makes the most practical wrapper for everyday use; any lace garment should only be used very rarely as the baby may get his fingers or toes trapped in the holes. Several bibs will be needed for the baby's very messy meals. Many mothers use "going out" sets when they take the baby outdoors; these consist of jackets, bonnets and leggings, and may include woollen bootees or knitted gloves. However, a much more practical garment to keep a baby warm is a one-piece suit of stretchable material which will get bigger as the baby grows. A similar garment can be used at night or a sleeping bag, which is very warm and will replace most of the bedclothes mentioned in the last chapter.

Washing Clothes

As so many babies' clothes are now made of mixtures of synthetic materials and cotton, they are easily washable and can quite simply be put in the washing machine, either at home or in the launderette. When one is choosing clothes it is a good idea to ask the shop if they can be washed easily.

The difficulty of washing wool has made this material much less popular than it used to be. If you must use wool, the garment should be washed in warm soapy water and squeezed, not rubbed. Only soap flakes or a soapless detergent should be used and when the garment is clean it should be rinsed twice in warm clean water. The clean garment should be dried as quickly as possible, preferably flat and in the open air. If garments are allowed to dry slowly they tend to shrink and to get out of shape. Remember that hot water, rubbing with soap, and remaining wet for a long time will shrink wool.

Nappies

There are now many kinds of nappies, but the most common type is the terry-towelling square. The muslin squares are soft and may be used as liners but are not generally necessary. However, there are now some new types of nappy liners, which are better than muslin. A one-way nappy liner can be used to keep the baby dry; disposable liners are useful when the mother cannot wash them.

There are disposable nappies as well as disposable liners, but their cost means that they cannot be used very frequently. Many mothers find them useful when travelling or on holiday, but cannot afford them all the time.

Plastic pants are often used to cover the nappy. Although they are useful when going out, they may encourage nappy rash and should not be used continually.

Putting on Nappies

There are at least two ways of putting on nappies and these are shown in the diagrams. The nappy can be folded into a triangle, placing the apex of the triangle between the baby's legs and fastening the three ends with a safety pin placed horizontally.

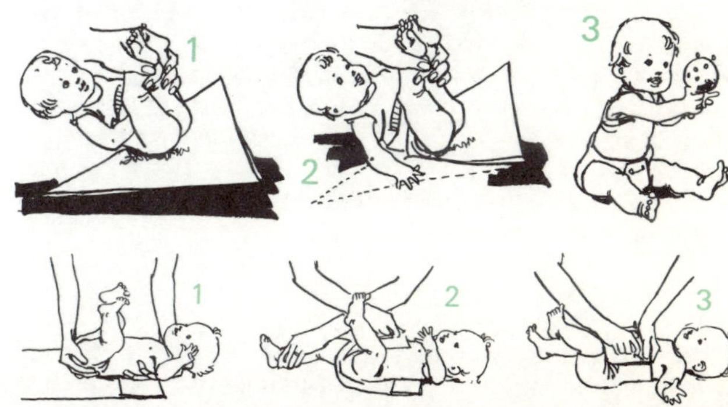

An alternative method is to fold the nappy in half, placing it between the baby's legs and pinning it together on each side of his waist. Always remember to close a safety pin when you unpin a baby's nappy.

Changing Nappies

It is an important rule to change a baby's nappy whenever it is wet or dirty. Clean the buttocks with soap and water and dry carefully. You can apply a mild ointment or cream, such as zinc and castor oil ointment, and this must be done if there is any sign of a rash.

The time for a baby to start using a pot is when he is old enough to sit on it alone—usually at about the age of 15 months. He usually learns to indicate when he wants to pass water and you should attend to him immediately he asks. If you are left to look after a baby, always ask his mother what sign he makes so that you can attend to him promptly.

Always wash your hands before and after attending to the baby or changing his nappy.

Washing Nappies

Wet nappies should be put straight into a pail of cold water; soiled nappies should be shaken out over the lavatory, scrubbed under running water and then put into a bucket of cold water.

After soaking, the nappies should be washed well in hot soapy water. Some doctors feel that synthetic detergents can damage a baby's skin and it is probably wiser to use soap flakes only. When the nappies have been washed they should be rinsed twice in hot clean water and boiled in clean water before they are hung up to dry. It is not necessary to boil the nappies if they are washed in very hot water in a washing machine. In a small flat it is often difficult to dry nappies and a spin dryer, drying cabinet, or tumbler dryer are very useful indeed.

Although this is the common way of cleaning nappies many mothers now use a product such as Napisan which is a chemical solution that cleans and deodorizes the nappies. The nappies are soaked for at least two hours, but preferably over-night, in a bucket of the solution and they are then thoroughly rinsed several times and dried.

Cleaning nappies can never be a pleasant procedure, but it is now much easier because many families have washing machines or a launderette near by. The nappies must always be rinsed before putting them in a washing machine. In some large cities there are firms who specialize in the laundering of nappies and, although their service is expensive, it will save the baby's mother a lot of hard and unpleasant work.

The Perambulator

The pram should be well sprung, easy to clean, shallow and provided with a safety strap and a foot brake. Most prams have metal bodies which are upholstered and lined with an easily cleaned material. The hood and mackintosh cover of the pram should only be used to screen the baby from rain, wind or sun. At other times the hood should be put up when the baby is not in the pram, to prevent the material cracking in the folds. Remember to have a net over the pram when the baby is sleeping in the garden, it will protect the baby from animals such as cats.

The pram is a necessity in most households. It is not the place, however, where a baby should sleep at night or spend most of his day.

The carry cot was mentioned in the last chapter. It is a very useful item and can be turned into a pram when put onto a frame with wheels.

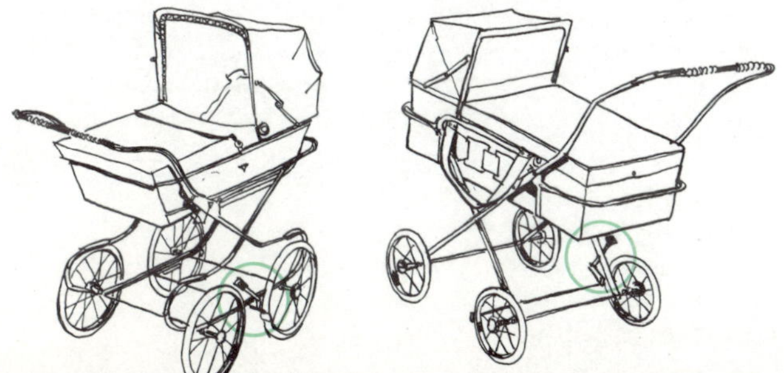

When the baby is older he will probably need a pushchair, but an alternative method of carrying him is in a sling. Carrying slings have become very popular recently and there are many types, some to carry the baby on the back, some to carry the baby on the side of the body. Some mothers keep the baby in a sling so that he can be carried around with her while she is working in the house.

The new-born baby

The new-born baby is a completely new individual with his own developing character and physical attributes.

In appearance he is pink with a soft skin, and he lies with his limbs folded up close to his body, in the same position as he was in his mother's uterus.

He has soft hair, variable in amount and colour from baby to baby, and this is replaced later by other hair, perhaps of a different colour.

Most British babies have blue eyes at birth but the eyes may change colour later. They keep them closed most of the time and when they open them gaze vaguely around, but by about five weeks they start to watch their mothers and may smile at them.

The new baby moves his limbs about aimlessly and although he cannot pick up objects with his hands he grips tightly if a finger is put in his fist.

The baby gets his food by sucking and once this action is established he may even suck his own fingers.

The baby's abdomen, or belly, is larger in comparison to the chest and the umbilicus (navel) has normally healed by the time the baby is 10 days to 2 weeks old.

His head is larger in comparison to the body than that of an adult and there is a small soft area on the top of the head where four of the skull bones have not yet fused, this is called the fontanelle and normally has closed by the time the baby is about eighteen months old. There is no need to be nervous of touching or washing this part of the scalp.

Length

The new-born baby is about 54 centimetres (21 inches) long. At one year he measures about 75 centimetres (29 inches).

Weight

The average new-born baby is about 3,400 grams ($7\frac{1}{2}$ lb) in weight, but often weighs between 2,500 grams and 4,500 grams. Babies who weigh less than 2,500 grams ($5\frac{1}{2}$ lb) at birth are called "babies of low birth weight" and usually need special care during the first few months of life.

An infant may lose up to 300 grams (6 oz) in weight during the first 10 days of life, but after this he will gain a steady 150 to 200 grams a week until by the age of 5 months he weighs about 7 kilograms (15 lb).

From then until the age of one year he will gain about 100 grams a week and by the time he is one year old will weigh approximately 9·5 kilograms (21 lb). A baby may not gain weight regularly each week, but provided he is taking his feeds, sleeping well, and is happy and contented there is no need to worry if for one or two weeks he gains less than usual.

Caring for the baby

Mothering

Babies need security and comfort. They get security by being held firmly and get warmth and comfort by being cuddled and touched.

Although a baby need not be picked up every time he cries, he will need to be kissed and cuddled several times a day. A baby is a human being who needs affection as well as care; he is not a piece of mechanism asking no more than feeding, sleeping, bathing and changing.

Remember that babies vary in the amount of attention they need, depending on their temperament. Some babies cry for much longer in the day than other babies and they will need to be picked up and cuddled more often. The mother will have to adjust her day around the baby, and there are many babies who have bouts of evening crying, sometimes called colic, which means they will need a lot of attention during the hours from 6 o'clock to 10 o'clock in the evening. If the crying continues the Health Visitor should be consulted.

A baby learns from contact with the world about him. It is important to remember that cuddling a baby and talking to him, even before he can talk, is part of his education. He will learn what happiness and love are from the attention given to him from his mother. In addition, being held firmly and peacefully in his mother's arms, he will learn that there are some secure places in the world. Many babies when they cry need to be fed, but there are often other reasons for a baby crying. It is always important to check that the nappy is dry, if he seems uncomfortable.

Sleep

A baby grows very rapidly during the first year of his life. Not only is his body growing, but he is continually becoming aware of and learning new things. It is therefore essential that he gets long periods of sleep. For the first few months of his life the baby will only be awake while he is being fed or bathed and should spend all his day asleep in his cot or pram in the fresh air. He should be placed in a sheltered part of the garden so that the sun does not shine on his face. If he has to be indoors, his cot should be placed by an open window. Most babies will sleep through a certain amount of noise, and there is no need to keep the household quiet just because the baby is asleep.

A baby of six months of age takes about 18 hours sleep; a year-old baby takes 15 hours. Except for the 10 p.m. feed and when his nappy is changed the child up to the age of one year usually takes 12 hours unbroken rest at night and this means sleeping from 6 p.m. to 6 a.m. Babies are usually put to bed at the same time each night so that they get into the habit of going to sleep at that time.

Stools

The stools passed during the first few days of life are a dark greenish brown in colour and of a tarry consistency. By the time a baby is ten days old they will have become mustard yellow in colour and the consistency of a soft ointment. They will remain like this, and two to three stools will be passed daily while the baby is breast-fed. Some breast-fed babies, however, only pass a stool every other day. Provided the motion is soft and yellow, this does not matter and the baby should not be given an aperient. When a baby reaches the age of three to four months, and starts to have other foods besides breast milk, his motions will become darker in colour and more formed until by the time he is one year old they will resemble an adult motion.

Activity

The new-born baby will spend most of his time asleep and even when he is awake will not move very much. He may cry, but cannot turn over in his cot or kick off the bed clothes. He will wave his arms about aimlessly and will grasp a finger if put in the palm of his hand. He may also draw his legs up when he cries. He cannot hold up his head until he is about three or four months old, nor sit up till six months. A baby's hearing is good and he will start or cry at a loud, sudden noise. By the age of one month he can usually distinguish between pleasant and unpleasant sounds. Although a baby's movements seem purposeless they have, in fact, a meaning and a use. In waving his arms and moving his legs, he is learning to use his muscles, to co-ordinate and give purpose to them and to understand space and distance. In crying, he is learning to understand sounds and is practising the movements which will later train him to talk. He is listening to the sounds around him and gradually learning to attach a meaning to each of them.

Skin

A baby's skin is smooth, soft and delicate. It must always be remembered that with the tiny baby it is very easy to rub off the top layer of the skin, and it will become red and sore and easily infected. A baby should therefore always be dabbed gently with a soft towel after his bath until the skin is quite dry. His skin should never be rubbed. His buttocks should be carefully sponged and then dabbed dry when he is changed—they should not be rubbed with the nappy, for this quickly damages the delicate skin and makes the buttocks sore.

Bathing the baby

The following will be required for bathing a baby:

A warm room as free from draughts as possible. One way of preventing draughts may be to use a screen.

A baby bath, usually of plastic, which is deep enough for the baby to splash about in. The bath should be put on a stand and should not be placed on the floor. There are some very useful baby baths which can be put over the family bath.

A low chair for the mother.

Soap dish which is sometimes attached to the bath stand.

Baby soap.

2 soft cloths. One of these will be needed for the face and one for the body.

A large towel.

Clean clothes.

Nappies.

Apron to protect the mother.

Bucket for soiled clothes and a paper bag for soiled swabs.

Toilet items. These include baby cream and powder, zinc and castor oil ointment and olive oil. Some cotton wool will also be needed to clean the nappy area.

A table or trolley.

Box or container for the toilet items.

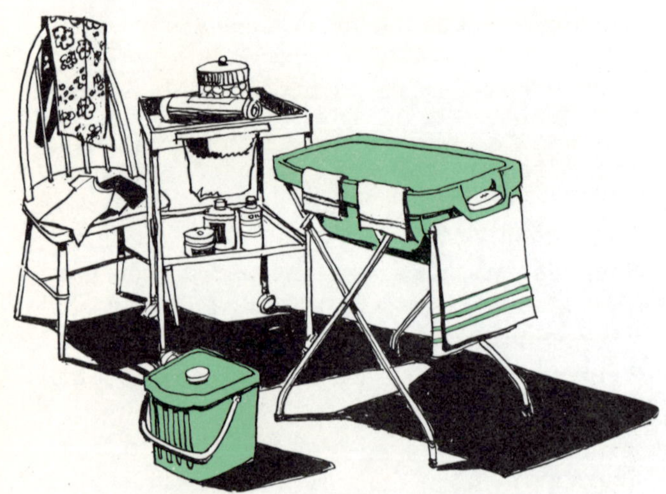

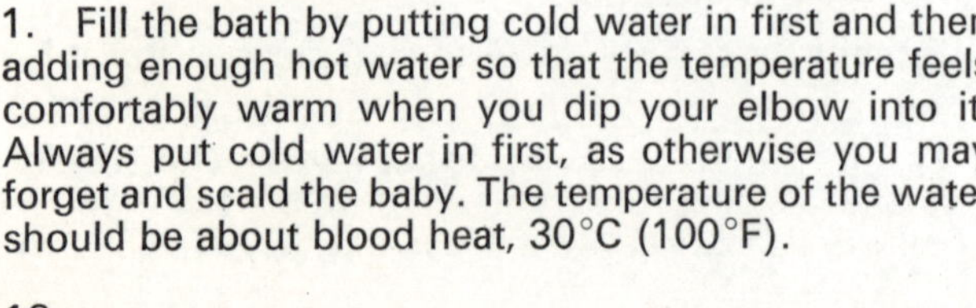

1. Fill the bath by putting cold water in first and then adding enough hot water so that the temperature feels comfortably warm when you dip your elbow into it. Always put cold water in first, as otherwise you may forget and scald the baby. The temperature of the water should be about blood heat, 30°C (100°F).

2. Undress the baby. Wash the face with clean water and pat it dry. It is helpful to wrap the baby in a towel enclosing his arms while you are washing his face and head.

3. Unless the nose is clogged, leave it alone. If it is dirty, clean it with a little twist of cotton wool. Leave the ears and eyes alone.

4. Now wash the head using a little soap and massage the scalp with your hands. Rinse away the soap and dry. If the scalp is scurfy, use a good shampoo containing cetrimide. After the bath you can also rub olive oil into a scurfy scalp.

5. Soap the baby all over by using the palm of the hand or a soft flannel.

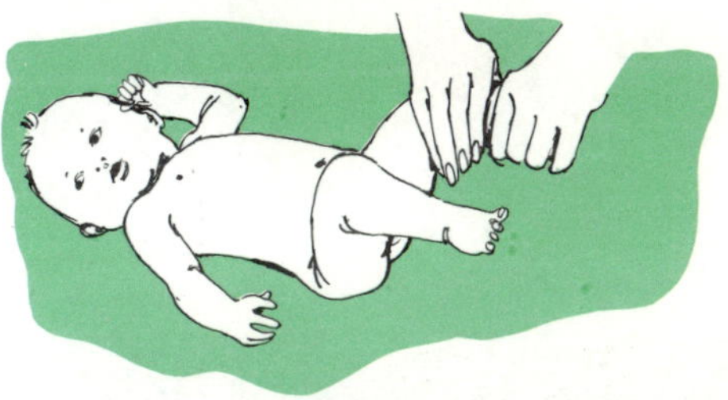

6. Place the baby in the bath, holding him firmly with your left hand in his left arm pit and your right hand under the buttocks.

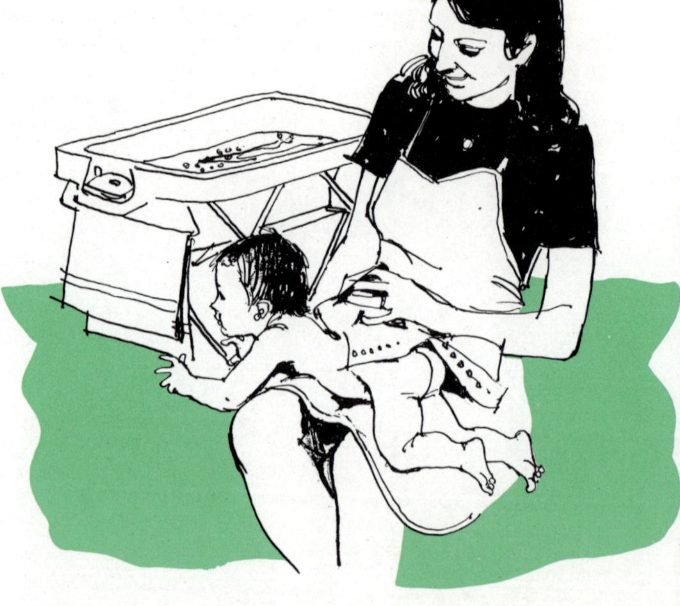

7. Still supporting the baby, rinse off the soap.
8. Take him out and pat him dry on your lap or on the table. Pay special attention to the folds and creases of the body. If you do not dry them properly they may become sore. Never rub a baby dry, pat him dry. You may use a little powder to make him smell sweet, but powder must not be used instead of drying.

Feeding

During the first few months of life a baby tends to spend the day sleeping and eating. Many babies take a feed about every four hours, but if the baby is small he will often cry for food more frequently, about every three hours. In recent years, there has been a tendency to depart from the absolutely regular routine of feeding a baby every three or four hours and to let him choose his time of feeding for himself. This will mean that the mother must get to know when her baby is hungry by the way he cries. In any case a baby should not be treated as a machine, but as an individual who quite early shows likes and dislikes, who requires both security and affection and who does not always want to feed at the same time and have the same quantity of food.

The baby who is taking his food approximately every 4 hours will probably feed at 6 a.m., 10 a.m., 2 p.m., 6 p.m., and 10 p.m. There may be another feed at 2 a.m., until he is about 6 weeks old. No mother should ever hesitate to feed a baby if he wakes earlier than the usual time, nor need she worry to wake him up if he is still asleep when his usual feeding time comes round. At some time during the day, probably in the morning, the baby will need his vitamin A, C and D, unless he has specially fortified milk.

Feeds

During the time of feeding, the baby should have his mother's undivided attention, whether he is being fed on the breast or by bottle. He will not feed well unless he feels secure and he should therefore be held comfortably in his mother's lap with his head supported in the bend of her elbow. The mother should be sitting comfortably in a low chair. If the baby is bottle fed, the routine is the same and the baby should be held comfortably and securely in the arms and the bottle held while he is sucking. The bottle should be held so that the teat is lower than the end of the bottle so that there is no air in the teat. If there is air in the teat, he will swallow the air, which will fill his stomach with the result that he will be less hungry in the middle of the feed and will stop sucking. It is bad practice to put the bottle in the baby's cot and let him feed himself because this can easily cause ear infections or asphyxia.

If he takes about 15 minutes, about half way through there should be an interval while the baby rests against the shoulder and has his back gently rubbed so as to bring up wind. Another way of bringing up wind is for the mother to sit the baby up on her lap and pat his back. This is often done again at the end of the feed. If the baby does not belch within 5-10 minutes it is not necessary to go on winding him for a long time, as it means there is no air in his stomach.

After the feed it is nice for the baby to have a period when he is cuddled in his mother's arms and talked to, so that he can go off to sleep and then be returned to his cot.

Breast Feeding

During the time that a mother is carrying a baby in her womb, her body is preparing to feed him when he is born. Her breasts become larger and produce milk. A few hours after the baby is born he is put to his mother's breasts and sucks the milk which she creates. Of course, the human being is not the only animal to feed babies at the breast and you will have seen many other animals suckling their young. The milk which a mother manufactures in her breasts for her baby is particularly suitable for the human child. It differs in its constitution from any other kind of milk and it contains the substances essential for growth, health and protection from disease and it is moreover already warm. It is perfectly true that there are other foods on which babies will thrive, but the best food for a baby is breast milk. It is also safe food, because it is not exposed to the risk of contamination and is free from harmful germs.

To feed a baby well, the mother must have a good diet of fresh fruit and vegetables, fish and meat, eggs and plenty of milk. A baby is usually breast fed every three or four hours during the day. During the time a mother is feeding her baby she must have peace, quiet and rest, and strain or worry must be avoided. Breast feeding is most important during the first three months and can be continued until six to eight months.

Many mothers are worried because they think their milk looks watery. It is important to remember that human milk is different from cow's milk and one must not expect it to look the same. Human milk looks pale and weak, but it is specially made for human babies whereas cow's milk is made for calves and needs to be adapted before being fed to human babies.

Bottle Feeding

There are occasions when a mother is unable to feed her baby herself or does not want to. Although breast feeding gives many women a lot of pleasure and is certainly the most convenient way of feeding a baby,

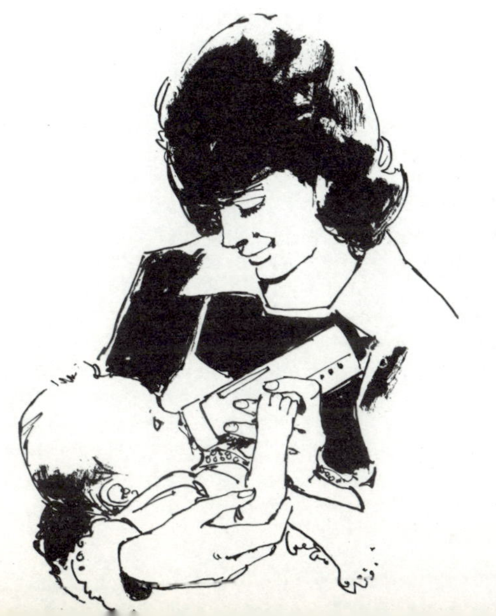

it is important to remember that bottle feeding is perfectly satisfactory. A baby will thrive on one of the modern adaptations of cow's milk which are specially prepared for infants. There are three alternatives which are usually available—

Dried milk. Dried milk powder is almost sterile and the curd is softer than that of liquid cow's milk. This makes it easier for the baby to digest. Dried milk is readily stored and carried about and does not turn sour in hot summer weather.

There are different brands of dried milk but they are all very similar and most firms manufacture two types, "half cream" and "full cream" dried milk.

Half cream dried milk has had some of the fat or cream removed from the milk before it is dried. This makes it easier for the very small baby to digest, and it is used during the first few weeks of life. Full cream dried milk has had no cream removed before it is dried. This milk is used for most babies after two to three weeks of age.

A packet of dried milk contains a spoon called a "measure" and one measure of dried milk is mixed with 30 millilitres (1 fluid ounce) of water. It is important to measure the milk powder very carefully as a milk which is made up incorrectly can be very dangerous to a baby. In particular, the milk powder should not be packed into the measure and the measure must be carefully levelled off before being mixed with the water. Some milks must have sugar added; the amount is stated on the packet. It is usually about 1 teaspoonful per feed.

Evaporated milk (unsweetened). Evaporated milk is cow's milk which has been heated to a high temperature in a vacuum so that some of the water is evaporated; a concentrated milk is left which is canned in sterile air-tight tins. This milk is sterile and easy for the baby to digest. One measure of evaporated milk is mixed with 2½ measures of water and with a measured amount of sugar. As the baby grows the milk can be made more concentrated; follow the instructions on the tin. Never use sweetened condensed milk for a baby.

Liquid cow's milk. Cow's milk contains germs which may be harmful to a baby. You should therefore choose a milk which has been pasteurized; this means that it has been heated and cooled sufficiently to kill all the harmful germs. There will be a label on the bottle stating that the milk has been pasteurized. In any case all liquid milk for feeding babies should be boiled before being used until the baby is one year of age. Boil milk in a clean saucepan and then pour into a jug which has also been boiled to render it free from germs. The jug must be covered with a saucer which has been boiled, and it can then be rested in a basin of cold water or put in a refrigerator.

It is a golden rule that all milk must be kept clean, cool and covered and it is not sufficient to cover milk with a piece of muslin or linen. Germs and dust can get through this.

In 24 hours a baby takes about 165 millilitres for each kilogram of his body weight (2½ ounces for each pound of weight), so you must know the baby's weight. Take for example a baby weighing 5 kilograms (11 lb). He will need at least $5 \times 165 = 825$ millilitres of milk in 24 hours. He takes five feeds every 24 hours and therefore takes about 165 millilitres (5½ fluid ounces) at each feed. Remember that every baby is an individual and one baby may drink a lot of milk whereas another may take less, but so long as a baby is contented and gaining weight there is nothing to worry about.

If liquid cow's milk is being used it will be necessary to add water and sugar to make it suitable for a baby's digestion. Half milk and half water should be given until the baby is two or three weeks old, two-thirds milk and one-third water from three weeks to four months, and full-strength milk after this. Sugar is added in varying amounts from one teaspoonful per feed for a month old baby to three teaspoonfuls per feed for a six month old baby.

Vitamins

Babies need vitamins. Vitamin A prevents night-blindness and some forms of dry skin, Vitamin D prevents rickets and Vitamin C prevents scurvy. Many modern artificial milks have added vitamins as well as an addition of iron. However, most babies will need a small addition of vitamins to their diet every day to make sure that they get enough. This can be done by giving the Vitamin A, C, and D drops which are available at any Child Health Centre. The dose mentioned on the outside of the bottle should be given and should not be exceeded as large amounts of vitamins can be dangerous.

Preparation of a feed

Before preparing a baby's feed you must wash your hands, with soap and water, and dry them on a clean towel. Have everything ready on a table. First of all make sure that the utensils have been adequately sterilized.

Sterilization

There are two main methods of sterilization, boiling and hypochlorite solution.

(a) **Boiling.** This has already been mentioned in the previous chapter. In order to kill the germs it is important that the utensils should be immersed completely in boiling water and boiled for 3 minutes. It is important to remember that you must boil all the utensils you are going to use, including spoons and jug covers.

(b) **Hypochlorite Solution.** This is a very satisfactory method of sterilizing utensils in the home. You will need a large container for the solution; as hypochlorite corrodes metal, the container must be plastic, glass or china and any spoons used must be plastic. When all the utensils are clean they can be immersed completely in the solution and left until the next feed. They must stay at least two hours in the solution, and it is important to make sure there are no bubbles left in the bottle or the teat. In particular, it is important to make sure there is not a bubble left in the teat hole so the solution should be squirted through the hole before immersing it in the solution. The bottle and teat must be completely clean, as any milk left on the inside will prevent the solution working.

Making up the feed

If you are using a dried milk, place the required numbers of measures of food in a jug which has been sterilized. Add a little of the hot boiled water to make a smooth cream and then make up with the hot boiled water to the specified amount, stirring well all the time you are adding the water. If you are using liquid cow's milk or evaporated milk, pour the required amount of milk and water into a clean saucepan. The water should come from the drinking tap. Bring the mixture to the boil and add the required amount of water, stirring well with a spoon that has been sterilized by boiling. Now pour it into a jug which has also been sterilized.

Cover the jug with a sterilized inverted saucer and keep it in a cool, clean place or a refrigerator.

It is best to make up one feed at a time. If you make up more than one feed you must be very careful to keep the mixture free from contamination, if possible in a refrigerator, until the time for the next feed. When you want to feed the baby, measure out the correct amount of feed into the feeding bottle and place it in a jug of hot water and keep it there for ten minutes. This will heat the milk to the right temperature for the baby. If it feels comfortably warm when a drop of milk is shaken onto the back of the hand, the temperature will be all right.

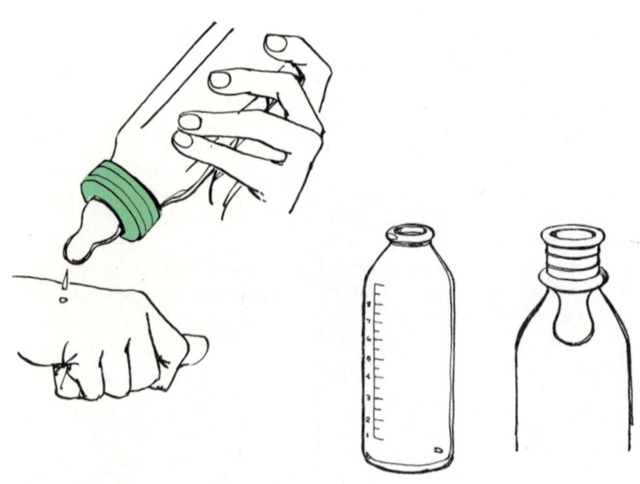

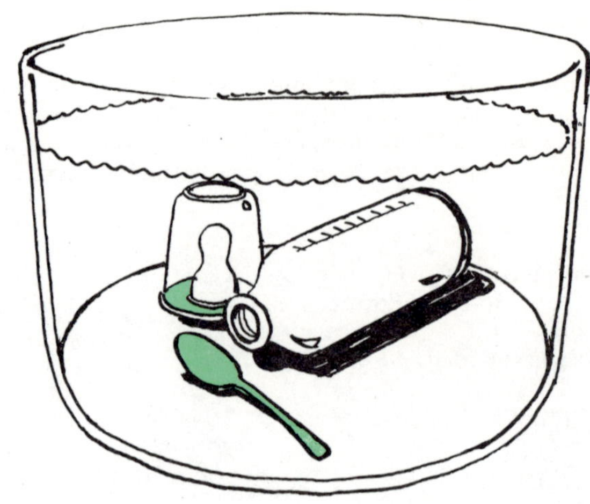

Bottles

The usual type of bottle used today is an upright, unbreakable one. It is useful to have a bottle with a wide neck so that it can be easily cleaned and the teat is often included in a plastic screw cap, which means it can be easily fitted on to the bottle. There are some disposable feeds available, in which the milk can be bought already mixed in the bottle which is then thrown away after the feed.

The bottle of milk can be kept warm for the feed by placing it in hot water but there are also some electric warmers available on the market.

Care of bottles

After each feed place the bottle in cold water, then wash with hot water, rinse well, and stand it upside down to drain. If you are using the hypochlorite method of sterilization, the bottles can then be put in the solution until they are next needed. If you are using the boiling method of sterilization, you can save the bottles and sterilize them once a day by putting them in a pan of cold water with the spoon which you are using for stirring, and sterilize by bringing the whole pan to the boil. When the pan has boiled for 3 minutes it can be taken off the heat and the bottles allowed to cool.

Care of Teats

Rub the teats inside and out with salt, rinse them in cold water and then sterilize them in hypochlorite solution or by boiling them. They can be kept either in the solution or, after boiling, in a clean covered jar which is boiled daily.

Remember, if ever you are left in charge of a baby and have to prepare his feed, you must follow all the instructions for sterilization faithfully, for if you are careless in making up a feed the baby might become infected and seriously ill. Once you learn the proper routine for preparing a baby's feed, you will find it very simple and easy. Be sure that you are told how to make up the feed, that is, how much milk powder, evaporated or liquid milk, water or sugar are to be added. Also enquire if you are to give the baby any vitamin drops, and if so how much.

Food poisoning

If food is not eaten when it is fresh or if it is not properly kept, it is liable to cause "food poisoning".

Symptoms of this condition are a general feeling of illness, pain in the stomach, nausea and vomiting. Sometimes there may be diarrhoea.

Food poisoning is usually due to germs which have contaminated the food. Therefore, food must always be prepared with clean hands and must be kept clean, cool and covered. It should be eaten as soon as possible after it has been prepared. In this way food poisoning can be prevented, for it is almost always caused by germs introduced into the food by people who have been careless and dirty in its preparation.

Remember that evaporated milk can easily become contaminated when the tin has been opened. An opened tin of evaporated milk should always be kept in a refrigerator and must be thrown away if it has not been used within 24 hours.

Weaning and diet

Weaning

Weaning means taking a child off breast feeding and feeding it by some other means. Nowadays, however, the term "wean" is used for the gradual introduction of solid foods to a baby's diet, whether the baby is fed on the breast or on the bottle. It is usual to start adding to the diet from three to four months onwards, although there has been a tendency recently to add solid foods at an earlier age. Early weaning may not be satisfactory as it can easily make a baby fat and should only be introduced on the advice of a Doctor or Health Visitor.

Weaning takes place over a period of months, various foods being added to the diet one at a time. At first they are given in very small quantities—not more than a taste. If the baby likes the new food and digests it well, showing no stomach or bowel upset, then the new food is continued. If not, it is usual to wait a week or two and then to try again.

Weaning is completed at about nine months, and then the baby's feeds will be reduced from five a day to three; finally he is having his meals sitting in his own chair.

It is best to give the additional foodstuffs to a baby in a spoon instead of adding them to a bottle feed. In this way bottles are avoided and the baby learns at an early age to accept food other than from the breast or from the bottle.

Only one new food should be added at a time, and then given in very small quantities. At the age of three

months one could try a little red gravy from the joint before a two o'clock feed. A little later a quarter to half a teaspoonful of egg yolk can be given two or three times a week, or one of the proprietary cereal foods. Many mothers now start weaning with a cereal but this requires a lot of care because of the danger of making the baby fat.

Diet from birth to one year

Foods consist of proteins, fats, carbohydrates, vitamins, minerals and water. Each of these substances has a definite part to play in the growth of a healthy baby.

Proteins. Proteins are the body-building factors which are necessary for growth. The best proteins are obtained from meat, fish, milk, cheese and eggs. Other proteins, not of quite the same value, can be obtained from fruits and vegetables. The baby derives most of his proteins from milk and eggs and this is one of the reasons why milk is so important to a young baby.

Fats. Fats are derived in infancy chiefly from the creamy portion of milk, but later on are obtained from meat and fish. A baby uses fat to store up his energy.

Carbohydrates. Carbohydrates are derived from sugars, vegetables and cereals, and they form the main source of quick energy. It will be seen therefore that you need proteins in order to grow, fats in order to keep you warm and to have a store of energy, and carbohydrates in order that you may always be active.

Vitamins. Proteins, fats and carbohydrates are not in themselves sufficient. We need substances called "vitamins" to keep us healthy and to prevent disease. To have strong bones and to avoid deforming diseases like rickets we need Vitamin D, found in butter, eggs, milk and, in particular, cod liver oil. Without enough Vitamin C we should develop an illness called scurvy; this vitamin is found in fruit and fresh vegetables.

Mineral salts. Certain mineral salts are also necessary. Iron is needed for good, rich blood. Calcium for firm, strong bones.

Water. A large part of our body is made up of water, and therefore we must drink plenty of fluids, for we are losing water and sweat when we are active, when our bowels are open, or when we pass urine.

Food given to a small baby should be well chopped up, sieved, mashed or minced to make it smooth but, when teething commences, usually at about the age of seven months, the baby may be given a hard crust or a rusk to bite on.

The following foods are suitable for the weaning period:

1. meat gravy
2. egg yolk
3. sieved vegetables
4. cereals
5. purées
6. custard, jelly, blancmange, junket
7. grated cheese
8. whole egg
9. finely chopped or pounded white fish
10. minced fresh meat, liver, chicken, soft herring roes
11. buttered rusks with honey, golden syrup or seedless jam
12. thin sandwiches, sponge fingers, toast
13. mashed vegetables, for example potatoes, carrots, turnips, parsnips
14. toast with dripping or bread fried in bacon fat
15. fried bacon.

The foods numbered 1-8 will usually be well digested by a baby by the time he is six months, foods 9-13 by eight months, foods 14 and 15 by the age of one year. It is better to prepare the baby's foods oneself, but many mothers now use the strained foods in tins or jars which are specially prepared for babies. These foods are not as nutritious for babies as the ones that are home-produced, but they are undoubtedly very convenient.

Nearly all the essentials of a good diet are found in normal varied meals. However, as there may be a deficiency of Vitamin D and C, babies are usually given extra amounts of these vitamins in drops or in the form of cod liver oil and orange juice.

If you are left to look after a baby, ask for a complete list of all that the baby should eat while you are in charge and how it should be prepared. Never give a baby anything else.

One year's progress

The normal, healthy baby has a clear skin, bright eyes, rosy cheeks and pink lips. He is happy and contented and sleeps well and peacefully. He is ready for his meals and digests them easily, his bowels are open regularly, and his stools are soft and inoffensive. Growth, both physical and mental, proceeds smoothly and, by the time the infant is one year old, he can stand up and say a few words.

Remember, however, that every child is an individual and will not grow or behave exactly according to plan. For example: the babies of tall parents tend to be heavier and longer than those of small parents; an infant who is continuously with adults will learn to speak more quickly than one who spends much of his time with babies of his own age; a baby may be quite healthy and only gain 50 grams (2 oz) in weight in one particular week; one infant may cut his first teeth at six months and another equally healthy baby may cut his first teeth at nine months or even later.

In the same way that the bodily growth of babies varies, so do their temperaments. A placid, contented baby may sleep most of the time between his meals; another more excitable, active infant may sometimes only sleep for one to two hours. Even tiny babies have definite likes and dislikes and allowances must be made for this; for example, a baby may refuse one kind of cereal, but take another which has a slightly different flavour.

The table of progress shows what to expect a baby to do at different ages, but remember that your particular baby will not necessarily fit in with these tables. Provided he is healthy and happy, having a good diet and plenty of sleep it does not matter if his first tooth has not appeared by the time he is ten months old or even a year old.

Children thrive best when they have the love and confidence of adults and they learn by watching and imitating other children and adults. This method of learning may be helpful for mothers who want to teach their children hygiene. A child who always sees his parents wash their hands before a meal will soon learn to do the same. Even the tiny baby seems to know whether his home is really secure and will react to "atmosphere". He may refuse his feeds, not because he is ill but because there has been some upset in the house and his mother is anxious and worried. A secure and happy home is the best start in life that can be given to any baby and it is the place where he will have the greatest chance of remaining healthy and growing and developing normally.

Age in months	Weight Gain	Teeth	Sleep per day	Social Development	Activity	Remarks
1-2	Average weight at birth 3·5 kg., gain in weight 150-200 grams a week so that by the age of 2 months the baby would weight about 5 kg.	None	Most of the time except when feeding	Different cry to express pain or hunger. Cannot see clearly at first and eyes wander aimlessly, but by 5-6 weeks will gaze and smile at mother	When awake waves arms and legs in an aimless fashion. Grasps things when they are put in his hand. Can hold head erect for a few seconds when held against the shoulder	Fontanelle. This is a soft diamond shaped area on the top of the head where the bones have not yet joined. About 2 cm. (nearly 1 in.) in diameter
3-4	Weight gain 150-200 grams a week so that a baby who was 3·5 kg. at birth weighs 6 kg. at 4 months	None	About 20 hours	Smiles and makes noises and recognises his mother when she bends over his cot	Holds his head steady when held in his mother's arms. Tries to roll over when lying on his back. Plays with his fingers. Begins to follow a moving object with his eyes.	
6	Gaining about 150 grams a week and at 6 months weighs approximately 7·5 kg.	2 lower middle teeth (central incisors) may appear	About 18 hours	Recognises friends as well as his mother. Shows pleasure and displeasure by laughing or crying	Movements more co-ordinated and purposeful. Can reach out and grasp a toy with his hand. Plays with toes as well as fingers. Can sit up without support for a short time	Fontanelle still about 2 cm. in diameter. Suitable toys: ring and rattle. Diet: still breast fed or having a bottle, but has also been having some solid food for nearly 3 months
9	Gaining about 400 grams per month	6 teeth—usually 2 lower and 2 upper middle ones (lower and upper central incisors) and 2 more upper teeth	About 17-18 hours	May be trying to say "Mummy" and "Daddy"	Sits up alone. Crawls and may be trying to pull himself up on to his feet. Can be taught to crawl towards things he wants and to wave his hand	Suitable toys—washable soft toys, ring and rattle. Diet: drinking out of a cup, eating practically everything provided it is sieved, mashed or minced
12	200-300 grams per month	8-10	About 16 hours	Can say 2-3 words and understand the meaning of "Yes" and "No"	Just starting to walk but may still need to hold on to things. Playing with toys	Suitable toys—washable soft toys, bricks, toys that rattle or can be pushed. Fontanelle smaller with a diameter of about 1-2 cm. Fontanelle closes at about 18 months

Normal growth

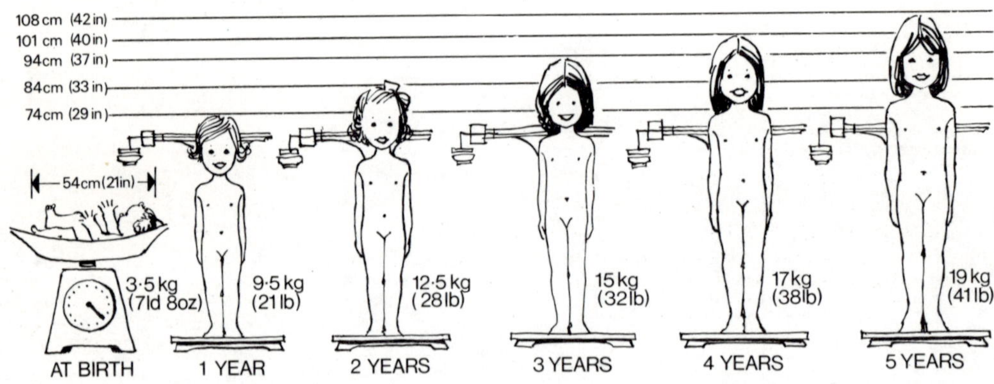

Weight

A baby who was 3·5 kilograms at birth and has been healthy during his first year usually weighs about 9·5 kilograms (21 lb) at one year old. After this, his gain in weight is slightly less each year; 3 kg (about 7 lb) from 1–2 years, 2·5 kg (about 5 lb) from 2–3 years, and 2 kg (about 4 lb) from 3–5 years. Thus by the age of 5 years he weighs 19 kilograms (41 lb). Normal children vary in their rate of gain in weight and although they should be weighed regularly, there is no cause for worry if the healthy child fails to gain weight for a month or two.

Height

At one year old a baby should measure about 74 centimetres (29 inches). During the next two years he will grow about 10 centimetres (4 inches) a year, so that at three years old he will measure about 94 centimetres (37 inches). After this he grows more slowly—about 12·5 centimetres (5 inches) between his second and fourth birthdays and then 5 centimetres (2 inches) each year. A child who measured 74 centimetres at one year will therefore measure 108 centimetres (42 inches) at five years. But remember that growth will be slower in an ill or under-nourished child, and even normal healthy children vary in their rate of growth.

Teeth

After a baby is born and before he actually cuts his teeth, his diet must be suitable for them to develop normally whilst they are in his gums. This is most easily ensured by proper food, either from the breast or one of the artificial milks. Like his mother it is important for him to get enough vitamin D and calcium.

The first tooth is usually cut about the seventh month, but even in quite healthy babies it may not arrive until the 11th or 12th month. The order of cutting varies, but in most cases the front teeth arrive before the back ones.

When weaning is begun and the baby starts to cut his teeth, he should be given hard crusts and rusks to bite on. Sweets and cakes between meals should not be given as they can upset the baby's appetite, make him fat, and also help to cause tooth decay.

The full set of twenty first teeth—also called "milk" or "baby" teeth—should have been "cut" by the time the baby is 2–2½ years old.

The routine of cleaning the teeth will be discussed later, but it should be started early enough for the child to have formed the habit by the time he is three years old. Cleaning the teeth alone will not keep them healthy: the child's diet must also be satisfactory.

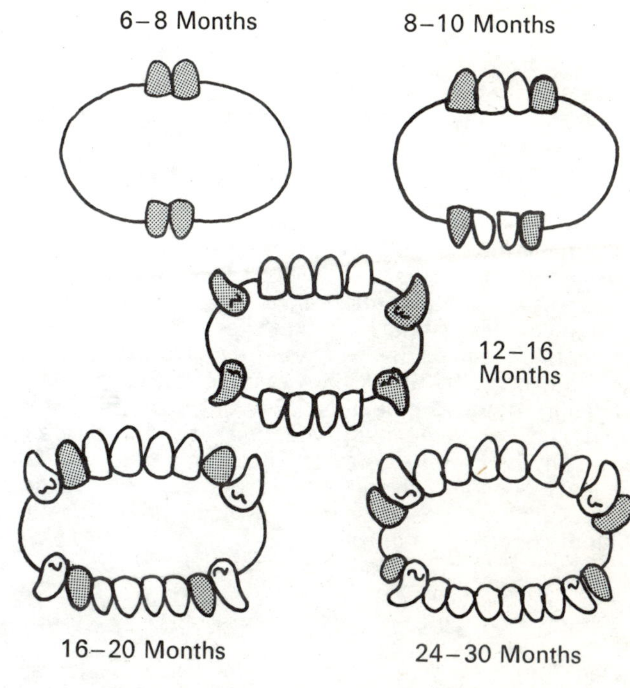

Last teeth to be cut are shown in Grey

Care of the young child

The 1 to 2 year old child must have enough of the correct foods if he is to become strong and healthy. He must eat enough of proteins, carbohydrates and fats, and will also need enough mineral salts and vitamins which are especially necessary for a growing child.

Pages 37-38 give specimen diets for the young child. These diets are not meant to show the exact amount of food which should be eaten by a child of a certain age, but rather the kinds of foods required and the approximate quantities taken by the normal child.

All children must have enough vitamin C and vitamin D. Vitamin C can be given in fresh fruit, green vegetables or a blackcurrant drink. The vitamin can also be given by using the government's A, C and D drops, and this can be used to give enough vitamin D to à child as well, unless he is having a cereal food containing vitamin D. At least one pint of milk should be taken daily, and milk drinks may be flavoured, for example, with tea, coffee, cocoa or chocolate.

The value of raw fruit for children must be stressed, not only does it provide vitamin C in the diet, but the chewing of a hard apple last thing at night, will also help to clean the teeth.

Meal-times should fit in with the family as far as possible, but they should always be peaceful and without distraction. The food should be attractively served and use made of different colourings. A pink blancmange is more attractive than a white one. With vegetables, colour may be obtained by the use of carrots, tomatoes, beetroot and greens.

Small helpings should be given and then a second helping if necessary. If the child is given too large a helping and then coaxed to finish it a meal-time can too easily develop into a battle between the child and his mother. Children take the amount of food they want and so long as they are taking a reasonable quantity of milk and a variety of other foods there is no need to worry about the diet. Too many parents insist on their children eating certain foods which are not completely necessary and then become upset when the children dislike or refuse them. Meal-times should be peaceful occasions and it is wise for adults to remember that they often dislike certain foods and they must expect their children to have likes and dislikes.

Some families have a tendency to be fat and the parents of such a family will need to be very careful with the diet of their children. Often it is helpful for the family to work out a family diet so that they can all remain slim. The main food which makes us fat is carbohydrate and it is a good idea to avoid large quantities of such food as bread, spaghetti, cake, biscuits, sugar or jam.

Specimen menus

1–2 years old

Breakfast

1 tablespoon of porridge or corn flakes or groats or Farex, or other cereal food.

1 boiled or scrambled egg, or
½ slice of bread fried in bacon fat with a small piece of bacon.

Bread, toast or rusk with butter and honey or seedless jam.

A glass of milk (250 millilitres or about 8 fluid ounces) to include that given with the cereal.

Lunch

½–1 tablespoon of minced meat or steamed or boiled fish.

1 tablespoon of mashed potatoes.

1 tablespoon of mashed or finely chopped vegetables (carrots, cabbage, spring greens, etc.) and

1 tablespoon of milk pudding with 1 tablespoon of stewed fruit (without skins or stones), or
1–2 tablespoons of blancmange, milk jelly, junket.

Water or orange juice to drink.

Tea

Thin bread and butter sandwiches with any of the following:

Honey or a seedless jam, grated cheese with Marmite, lettuce, tomatoes.

A portion of raw apple, small piece of plain cake or biscuit, a cup of milk (200–250 ml or about 6–8 fluid ounces).

2–3 years old

Breakfast

1–2 tablespoons of porridge or any cereal.

½ slice of bread fried in bacon fat and ½–1 rasher of bacon, or

1 egg boiled or scrambled.

Bread or toast and butter. Marmalade.

A glass of milk (250 ml or about 8 fluid ounces) to include that given with the cereal.

Lunch

1–1½ tablespoons minced meat, stewed steak, liver, sweetbread, boiled or steamed fish.

1 tablespoon boiled or mashed potatoes.

1 tablespoon vegetables (preferably green vegetables).

1–2 tablespoons of milk pudding with 1–2 tablespoons of stewed fruit, or

1–2 tablespoons of blancmange, milk jelly, junket.

Water to drink.

Tea

Bread and butter sandwiches with a filling of egg, sardine or cheese.

Plain cake or biscuit.

Fresh fruit.

A cup of milk (200–250 ml or about 6–8 fluid ounces)

Supper

A cup of milk may be given just before going to bed.

From 3 years onwards children will eat small portions of the usual family meals. Care should be taken to avoid too many fattening foods.

Clothing

The aim in clothing a young child is to keep him warm in winter and cool in summer while using the fewest and lightest garments possible. All his clothes should be light in weight, easy to launder, and those worn next to the skin should absorb moisture readily. They should be roomy, with wide armholes and good leg room to allow freedom of movement, and should fasten in front so that the child can learn to dress and undress himself at an early age.

Children should be taught to take reasonable care of their clothes, but they should not be dressed in elaborate expensive ones and expected to keep clean all the time. A child is learning while he is playing and should be dressed so that he can play happily with water and sand without being scolded for making his clothes grubby.

There are now many practical clothes for children available in the shops. Fashions have changed so that both boys and girls can now wear long trousers in the winter and do not get cold as they used to in the past. Cotton dungarees are useful garments both for small boys and small girls. They help to protect the clothes and allow the child plenty of freedom. Clothes should always be made of a material that will not catch fire easily and all party dresses and loose flimsy clothes should be made of flame-proof material.

Shoes can be made of leather, or canvas with rubber soles, a half inch longer than the foot and with a straight inner side. However, shoes are not always necessary indoors and, in a fully carpeted house, children are often best left to run around without shoes on.

Sleeping clothes should be of warm material in winter and a light material, such as cotton, in summer. The child also needs a warm dressing-gown and bedroom slippers.

For summer a boy will need a cotton vest and pants, a cotton T-shirt, long trousers, thin socks and sandals. In very hot weather one must remember how easily a child can get sunburnt and, particularly at the beginning of summer, he should only be allowed to go into the sun for short periods until he has developed a tan.

A small girl can wear similar clothes. She can wear a trouser suit, a dress, or a simple skirt and jumper.

For winter a child may need a warmer vest and pants, together with long trousers and a pullover. The child will also require a warm coat for outdoor wear and, in very cold weather, a pair of long woollen leggings or warm trousers.

If the weather is wet, a raincoat and rubber boots are useful, but the boots should be changed immediately the child comes indoors as they make the feet hot and damp with sweat.

Exercise

Small children require exercise in the open air, but too much exercise causes fatigue and the small child should not be taken for long walks. He will enjoy being taken out for short walks but will get most of his exercise playing in the garden. If there is no garden, the child should be taken out to a public park and allowed to play there for at least two hours daily.

Sleep

Small children take plenty of sleep and a child of 2 often sleeps for 12 hours a night and takes another hour's rest during the day. It is useful for "Going to bed" to be at the same time each night; it should not be hurried and the child must not get excited. He should be washed and undressed quietly and allowed to help in this. Many children like to be told a story or to have a tune sung to them before being finally tucked up for the night in a well-ventilated bedroom.

It is important to remember that children vary in the amount of sleep they need. Many children take much less sleep than others and there is no need to worry if a child sleeps for a shorter time than the figures mentioned. If he becomes tired from lack of sleep then he will sleep longer the next night.

Development 1 to 5 years

One year old

At one year most babies have learnt to take a few steps though they are still rather unsteady on their feet.

They will also begin to use simple words such as "Mum-mum" or "Da-da" and will understand the meaning of "yes" and "no".

One to two year old

At the age of 1½ years they can usually walk easily and have started to run. They enjoy pushing or pulling small wooden toys on wheels. At this age an infant still prefers to play alone or with an adult, rather than with other babies of his own age.

At two years a child is able to say short sentences, likes to listen to stories and can repeat short nursery rhymes, is able to throw a ball and is starting to climb.

Three year old

Some children are more backward in speech than others, but there is no need to worry unless there is considerable delay in saying at least some words. When talking to a young child simple words should be used but not "baby language"; if this is used too often he will copy it and not learn correct speech. When talking to a young child, remember to use words and sentences so that he will understand how to fit words together.

At 3 years the child can jump, dance and ride a tricycle and will enjoy helping his mother; he can answer simple questions and talk quite fluently.

Four to five year old

At 4–5 years he will enjoy playing with other children and can hold his own with them.

Play—Toys—Games

The mental development of a young child will depend largely on play and the amount of stimulation he is given by his parents. Learning and training is mostly through imitation and games, and the importance of "play" in the formation of a child's character is not always realised.

A baby when he starts to crawl will like toys that roll and make a noise. The one year old, who is trying to walk, will appreciate an animal on wheels which he can push and which will help him to balance. A child up to 2 years will explore and feel things with his mouth as well as with his hands and will only gradually use a toy in the way in which it was intended to be used. He will enjoy large wooden toys that can be pushed or pulled along. The toys should be solid and well made so that they will not fall over or break.

A child of this age is not a sociable being and prefers to play alone or with one adult whom he knows. If a group of children of this age are put together with some toys, they will each take a toy and return to a corner of

the room and play alone. Attempts to make them share toys will only end in outbursts of temper and tears.

About the age of 2 years most children love to play with sand and water. They love paddling and sitting in the water or just splashing about in it.

Between 2 and 3 years of age, the child will start to play with smaller toys, and matching games such as post boxes. He will enjoy threading cotton reels on string and likes to hammer a peg board.

At 3 years old, play will be largely imitative, such as trying to copy adults and helping in the home. Washing doll's clothes, sweeping the floor with a toy brush and dustpan and helping father in the garden are all favourite games.

At 4 years of age, imagination plays an even greater part in the child's activities. He likes dressing up and the smallest item of clothing or equipment may allow a child to transform himself into something or somebody else. The small boy with a whistle is an engine—the small girl with a tinsel crown is a princess.

All small children from 2 years onwards need paint and crayons, plasticine or clay to play with. They should have the opportunity to be creative, however messy they may become in the process.

They also need the opportunity for physical activity and a large garden is the ideal playground for the small child. Here he can have a swing, be allowed to dig and have his own small patch of garden to cultivate, be given a tub or water to play in on warm days and be allowed to climb if there are suitable trees. When there is no garden available children should be taken out into a park daily, preferably to a children's playground where there are swings and a climbing frame.

Children under the age of 5 do not usually enjoy organised team games. Small boys will play happily together at cowboys and red indians; a group of small girls will play together at keeping house or "school"; they are too young to show any "team spirit". They will run races, skip or see who can jump the highest, but they are all competing as individuals—not as a team. The only type of team game or round game which a young child really enjoys is one in which he can sing or make a noise himself as well as being part of a team, for example "Gathering Nuts in May", "Oranges and Lemons" or "Ring-a-Roses".

Story-telling

All children love to be told or have stories read to them, especially at bed time. They like to hear the same one over and over again, but it must be the same each time and they will correct you at once if you have made any alterations in the tale.

Children love imaginative and dramatic stories and the story should be short with plenty of action and no long descriptions of scenery. They like fairy stories and tales about animals or toys which come magically to life. A small child imagines that even a chair or table can talk and he enjoys stories in which familiar objects speak and move.

Most children are too active to sit still and listen for very long and they enjoy a pause so that they can supply the next word. They enjoy acting one of the characters as you read the story.

Although children like exciting stories they should not be told frightening or horrifying tales and particularly not at bed time; a story about a wicked witch may be exciting when it is being read but, to the imaginative child, it may become too real when the light is turned out and he is trying to go to sleep.

Music

The infant of only a year old will listen to music and enjoy it, especially if it has a marked rhythm, and will even try to move in time to the music. Few children under the age of 5 can sit and listen to music. They will listen if they can be active at the same time, but the 4 or 5 year old will thoroughly enjoy taking part in a percussion band.

If you watch a mother singing a lullaby to her baby as he goes to sleep you will notice the evident pleasure of the infant, although he is still too small to sing himself. The child who frequently hears such songs will be able to sing simple tunes and nursery rhymes by the time he is 3 years old. He will enjoy singing in a group and singing "action" songs and will try to join in when his favourite nursery rhyme is played.

The child's love of moving in time to the music makes it easy for him to learn to dance. A 3 year old can learn simple dancing steps and a small girl of 4 will love to dress up and pretend she is a fairy dancing. Besides the enjoyment a small child gets out of dancing, it helps towards learning balance and control of movement. It is "fun", but it also teaches him to stand up straight and walk properly.

Principles of Health

It is always important to remember that it is better to prevent illness than to try and cure it when it occurs. Sometimes this involves special medical treatment, such as immunization which is given by injection, but there are other illnesses which can be prevented by simple cleanliness. Washing the hands before meals and brushing the teeth are two examples of measures which will prevent illness and which are simple to perform.

These good habits should be taught to children by example early in life, but it is important to do this patiently and repeatedly. Parents must themselves do the things they are trying to teach their children to do; a child will not bother to wash his own hands before a meal if he sees that his father never does this. Small children are quick to notice any hypocrisy in those older than themselves.

Washing

Children will need to be washed thoroughly at least once a day and this is usually done by taking a bath. However, most children will have to wash their hands and face several times in the day because it is very easy to get dirty. It is especially important to wash their hands after going to the lavatory and before meals. The reason for this is that infectious diarrhoea is usually caused by food which has been contaminated by dirty hands. The germs are often present in bowel motions and can be carried on the hands to the food unless there is a careful routine of hand washing after going to the lavatory. It is very important for the person preparing any food to have scrupulously clean hands before touching the food.

Bath time is in the mornings in some households, but in the evenings in others. Many families find that there is a general scramble in the mornings, in order to have breakfast and get off to work; bath time in the evenings before going to bed is probably a more convenient arrangement in these families. A child should be washed all over with particular attention being paid to hands and nails, knees, feet and between the toes where dead skin may collect and become smelly. Between the legs must not be forgotten, nor the neck or ears. A nail brush, soap and water are necessary for the hands, knees and feet of an active child. Soapy hands are sufficient for the young baby. Some people like flannels, but the hands are the easiest and most natural means of soaping and cleaning most of the body. It is of course best if the child can have a daily bath but, if this is not possible, he should be stripped and washed all over. The young child should be taught to wash himself, but he will need help and supervision from an adult. The hair will need brushing and combing; this should be done morning and evening and the hair should be washed at least weekly to make it clean. It is not just a question of looking tidy, because it does not matter if a child's hair is sometimes untidy and out of place, but it must be kept clean.

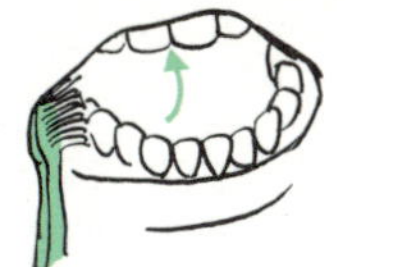

Up and down

Across biting surface

Brushing the teeth

Care of teeth should begin as soon as the first one appears. At first they should be wiped with a little cotton wool or brushed with a soft brush twice a day. As a child gets a little older tooth cleaning can be turned into a game and he can be encouraged to clean his teeth every morning and night. Like other good habits he will learn it more easily if he sees that both his parents are very careful in brushing their own teeth.

As soon as a child has a few teeth and can hold a small soft toothbrush, he should be given one and taught to use it. The back teeth as well as the front must be cleaned and they must be brushed upwards and downwards as well as sideways. The brushing is to remove small particles of food which lodge between the teeth; holes form in the teeth if bits of food are not removed and cause decay.

Bladder and bowels

The age at which children become "dry" varies considerably. Even when a child no longer needs a nappy during the day or at night, he may sometimes wet himself if he is particularly upset. Children will often wet their bed at night if they have been subjected to any mental strain or placed in new surroundings, and particularly if they have been separated from their parents. The arrival of a new baby causes jealousy and may result in bedwetting. If parents are patient with their children and sympathetic to their problems this wetting will improve without any special treatment.

There is a lot of disagreement about toilet training. One should always remember that most children cannot have control of their bowels or bladder until they are about 15 or 16 months. Many children are "potted" much younger than this and some may be very upset by the routine. It is usually more convenient to keep a child in nappies and not to worry about any form of "potty", at least not until the age of 15 months.

Children first of all learn to tell an adult that they have wetted or dirtied a nappy and want it changed; the next stage is that they will tell an adult just before they are about to wet themselves and they will go on from this to go to the pot or lavatory to pass urine when they feel it is necessary. During the period of learning control over their bladders, children will have many accidents and it is essential that they should not be scolded if they wet themselves. It is usual for control over the bladder during the day to develop earlier than during the night, so that a nappy may have to be worn at night until at least the age of 2 or 3. Nearly one in twenty children are still wet at night on many occasions at the age of 5 years, so that bed-wetting is a very common problem and it is not necessary to become anxious about it. If a child is still being wet at the age of 6 or 7 years, a doctor may be able to help by providing some treatment with a medicine or an alarm bell.

As a baby, the bowels are open many times a day; but this gradually becomes less frequent. When the toddler learns to use a pot during his second year he will probably open his bowels about once a day, but many children open their bowels more frequently and others may go one or two days without passing a motion. So long as the child's stools are soft and formed, without diarrhoea or very hard motions, there is nothing to worry about. Too often, children are given a purgative because they have not opened their bowels, although their stools are perfectly normal and they are in no discomfort. As a child is learning to control his bowels he will probably sometimes soil a nappy before he is able to tell his mother that he needs the pot. This needs patience and understanding from his parents and he must never be scolded. However, soiling that goes on for many years can be very worrying for parents and they should consult their doctor about it.

Common problems of Children

Fears

Certain new-born babies have certain instinctive fears. They are frightened by a sudden loud noise and they are very nervous if they are not held securely. However, most children who come from happy homes show remarkably little fear. They may even have to be taught for their own safety to be afraid of certain things, such as fire. They will often attempt tasks which appear dangerous to the person who is looking after them. Children learn by trial and error, and although they may fall and bruise themselves when they are trying to walk or climb, they will never learn unless we let them make mistakes. If they are told continually not to do something because they may hurt themselves, they will become nervous and, in the end, become too frightened to attempt anything on their own.

When you are left in charge of small children you must try never to appear frightened or worried. A child who has fallen down and cut his knee is both hurt and afraid. He needs to be reassured calmly that the pain will soon go and the bleeding stop, and his knee must be attended to quickly and quietly. If he is fussed over by someone who is worried and anxious, he will think that the injury is serious and become more frightened. All small children are, in many ways, helpless when they are left alone for they cannot feed or clothe themselves. For this reason, they are afraid of being alone and especially of being deserted by their mother. This fear is most marked in children who have had an unstable home and have at the back of their minds the thought that their parents may leave them. This fear becomes even greater at night when it is dark.

The child who is frightened of going to bed alone will often go to bed quite happily if his bedroom door is left open so that he can see his parents talking and moving around. The child's fears in the dark are very real and he should not be scolded or told he is being silly or babyish. This only makes him feel that you do not understand. Although he may cease to talk about his fears, he will feel even more lonely and isolated and may begin to have nightmares. If, however, you tell him that you know that he is a little frightened, but that he will hear you moving about or even that you will sit with him for a short while, he will feel more secure at once and will soon settle down to sleep. Some children are happier if there is a night-light in the room. They feel safer and its flicker fascinates them. For older children the shadows formed by a night-light may be frightening, but there are now many simple electric night-lights.

Children should never be told that if they are naughty "Mummy won't love you any more" or "will leave you". This frightens the child, he loses his sense of security and becomes even more difficult to manage. A child should know that his parents are always there and loving him even when he is naughty, so that he can be self-confident and unafraid. Such a child will go happily to other people while his parents are out and will not always want to cling to his mother.

Temper tantrums

Children, like adults, sometimes appear to start the day in a bad mood and refuse to do anything their parents want them to do. Such a child is often overtired or developing a cold and, if we recognise this fact and humour him a little, the day will pass without any outbursts of temper. This does not mean that we should spoil the child, but only that we should recognise that children as well as adults find it easier to be better tempered on some days than others.

There may be days, however, when the child appears to be good tempered and then suddenly gets cross over apparently nothing at all because he cannot get his own way over a trifling matter. He lies on the floor screaming and kicking in a "temper tantrum". Other children will "sulk". Most children go through this stage at the age of 2 to 5 years and it is part of the normal process of growing up.

Remember it is useless to get angry with a child whilst he is in a temper tantrum. He is already frightened by the violence of his own emotions and often wants to stop being cross or get out of his sulkiness but does not know how to do it. If his tantrum is ignored the child soon learns that he cannot get his own way by this means. Temper tantrums often occur in streets and in public places when the child knows that his parents will be embarrassed and likely to let him have his own way.

When the child has recovered from the temper tantrum he needs either comforting or punishment according to his temperament and condition. In any case, it is then the time to explain to him how silly he was to get so cross, and how little he achieved by doing so.

Jealousy

We all know how difficult the small boy or girl of 2 to 3 years may be when a "new baby" arrives. Although the child may say that he loves the baby, he starts demanding attention every time his mother starts to attend to the new baby, and refuses his food and cries at night. A child who has had control over his bowels may need nappies again. All this is his way of expressing the fact that he is jealous of the new baby who is taking up so much of his parent's time and attention.

The child does not want to be jealous or difficult but it is quite natural for him to behave in this way. Unfortunately the more difficult he becomes in his efforts to attract his parents' attention and love, the more he is likely to be scolded and the more he will blame the "new baby". Instead of being scolded he should be allowed to help look after the baby, who should always be referred to as "our baby".

He can fetch things for his mother when she is bathing or feeding the baby and should be praised and told how helpful he is to his parents. In this way he will soon learn to regard the baby as part of the family and will realise that it is his brother or sister and belongs to him as much as to his parents.

Feeding difficulty

Many small children go through a phase when they refuse to eat at home, but will enjoy their food if they visit a neighbour or friend. In fact, they will eat anywhere except at home, and the more trouble their mother takes over their food the more difficult they become. Such a child is not refusing food because he does not like it or is unwell, but he is staging a minor rebellion against his mother's authority.

Most children will get over this phase if it is ignored, but to do so is a test of the parents' patience and acting abilities. It is extremely difficult for parents to let a child refuse food regularly, and yet not to appear worried or concerned. If the parents can do this, in a short time the child will be eating and enjoying food again. All children, like adults, have their individual likes and dislikes in food, but these difficulties are usually overcome and only need a little imagination on the part of the adult who is preparing the food. A small boy who refuses to drink plain milk but likes cocoa should be allowed to have this and not forced to have unflavoured milk. The child who likes salads, but refuses greens, should be allowed to have his green vegetables as salads. It is of little use, however, expecting a child to eat something at table that an adult has just refused and one should not expect him to finish his greens when the adult sitting opposite him has not had any. Children are great imitators and if they see their parents eating normal, well balanced meals and not making a fuss about their food, they will soon learn to do the same.

Naughtiness

It is the duty of all parents to provide an environment in which a child can grow physically and mentally in normal conditions. He needs a quiet and happy home, but above all he must have security. He must be certain of the affection of his parents without being embarrassed by sentimentality. Parents must never quarrel in front of the child. It is a well known fact that most juvenile delinquents come from unhappy or insecure homes.

The average child from a good home may be naughty —but his naughtiness is superficial. He will be disobedient, lose his temper, tell lies, but he will learn not to do so as he grows older. He wants to be told what to do firmly and quietly and not scolded one day for what he was encouraged to do the day before. He needs an orderly routine and although he requires a certain amount of free-play, he does not want to decide what to do for himself all the time. The child who has not enough to do may be naughty because he soons learns that this is an effective way of attracting attention to himself. Boredom breeds naughtiness. A child who is happily occupied and whose parents are sufficiently interested in his play to direct it without interfering with his liberty, will be both happy and well-behaved. He may not be clean, tidy or quiet, but he is unlikely to be disobedient, destructive or unmanageable.

Accidents

Every year many children are injured or killed as a result of falls, asphyxia, burns, and scalds. Sometimes these accidents are caused in the home, sometimes in the street. Many could be avoided by a little care and foresight, so let us see how accidents occur and what we can do to prevent them.

In the first place, articles of furniture should be placed and fixed so that the child cannot pull them over onto himself.

Heavy, moveable articles should be completely out of the child's reach. Often an enticing ornament or a bottle of highly coloured fluid, perhaps a medicine, is just within a child's reach and he may pull it over onto his head.

Front doors must not be left open, so that young children can run out of the house into the street and be caught in traffic.

Cots must be designed so that a child cannot get his head between the bars. Windows must be guarded.

Children should be strapped securely into high-chairs or prams. There should, however, be sufficient movement to allow the child to feel free of any abnormal restrictions. In other words, security with the utmost freedom.

All these points may seem obvious, but thousands of accidents occur every year through ignorance and carelessness and from not taking the right precautions.

Poisoning

There are many dangerous poisons around any home. A child can quite easily die from swallowing a household bleach or one of the medicines, such as aspirin, which are used by most families. Treatment for poisoning is very unpleasant and usually requires admission to hospital, so it is much wiser to take elementary precautions to prevent poisoning. All medicines and drugs should be carefully locked away in a medicine cupboard which should be out of a child's reach and the key should be put somewhere which cannot be reached by a child, even when he climbs onto a chair. Similarly, common household substances, such as paraffin and bleach, should be put into a locked cupboard. No poisons should ever be put into a bottle that is usually used for drinks, such as a lemonade bottle. Poisons should be left in the poison bottle in which they are bought.

If you discover that a child has possibly taken a poisonous substance, do not delay but take him at once to a doctor or the casualty department of a hospital. They will be able to ring a Poisons Centre and find out exactly what treatment he requires.

Burns and Scalds

Burns and scalds are nearly always the result of someone's lack of foresight or carelessness. Young children should be told of the danger of fires and hot liquids. Teapots, cups and plates containing hot liquid should be put in the centre of the table and not near the edge where the slightest knock will upset them, and it is wise not to use a table cloth because it can be pulled by a small child.

Never carry a cup of tea or a pan of boiling water over a baby's head.

Around every fire or oil stove there must be a fireguard fixed so that the child cannot pull it away. Matches should be put right out of the child's reach. A night-light or candle in a room where a child is asleep must be well out of the child's reach, and it is probably safer to use an electric light. A child must not be allowed to play with highly inflammable toys.

If you are bathing a baby, put the cold water in the bath before the hot water, otherwise you may forget the cold water and scald the baby.

Never leave saucepans or kettles on the stove with a spout or handle pointing towards the room, unless it is well out of the child's reach. A child may pull on the handle and pour boiling water over himself. If possible, use one of the safety rings which can be clamped to the stove and will stop a child pulling a saucepan over.

Treatment

A burn or scald should immediately be immersed in cold water for ten minutes or until the pain ceases. It should then be covered with a sterile dressing as soon as possible to prevent it from becoming infected with germs. The dressing should be dry, for moisture is apt to spread infection. If you have not got a dry specially prepared dressing then a clean freshly laundered handkerchief will do. Do not remove clothes if a child has been seriously burnt, but get medical treatment immediately.

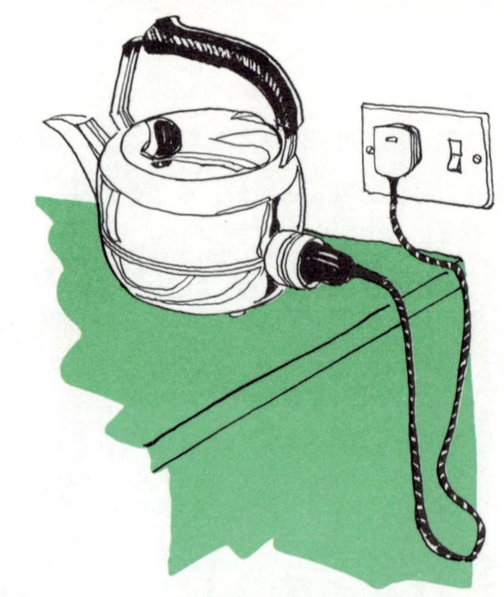

Electricity and gas

Children must be warned not to touch electric switches and gas taps. If possible, safety electric plugs should be installed throughout the house so that children cannot put their fingers in the sockets and electrocute themselves. If these cannot be used, electric switches and gas taps should be placed or guarded so that children cannot reach them and turn them on. A connecting plug on a wire for an electric kettle or iron should never be left dangling from a plug—it is possible for the child to put the plug into his mouth and get severe electric burns.

Asphyxia

After road deaths, this is the commonest method of accidental death in the under five year old. Pillows are dangerous and unnecessary for a baby. Plastic bags should never be given to a child to play with, for the child may pull the bag over his head and the plastic moulds itself to the shape of the face so quickly that it causes suffocation before the child can be rescued.

An unwanted refrigerator should never be left on a waste dump unless the door is taken off—several children have died after climbing inside an old refrigerator and finding themselves shut in.

Roads and Railways

Road accidents are unfortunately by far the largest cause of death in childhood. Children under 7 should never be allowed to cross a road unless they are with an adult or older person. Children going to school should cross the road at authorised pedestrian (or "Zebra") crossings where there is a person on duty to control the traffic. All children should learn the Green Cross Code and understand from the earliest age what a dangerous place a road is.

When travelling in a car an approved B.S. seat belt should always be used. A carry-cot should be carefully strapped to the back seat; young children need special seats bolted to the framework of the car into which they can be strapped, and older children will need special seat belts fitted on to the back seat of the car. Children should never travel with

their parents in the front of a car. Special safety catches should be installed on the car doors so that the back doors cannot be opened accidentally by a young child.

It is important to remember that railway tracks are dangerous places for children. It is easy for them to stray on to the track where they can be knocked down by the train or electrocuted by an electric rail. All railway tracks should be carefully fenced off and if the fencing is known to be unsafe the child should never be allowed near the track.

Drowning

A young child could drown himself in a small pond which is not very deep. Ponds should be fenced off from children or else they should never be allowed to go near a pond unless accompanied by an older person.

Responsibilities when left in charge of children

When you are asked to look after a baby or a young child, you must realise what an important job this is. You must take the job seriously and remember that you have care of the child until the parents return.

First of all, make sure you know the names of the child or children you are looking after. It is important for the parents to introduce them to you, so that they know who you are and are not frightened by being left with a stranger. Ask where the telephone is and make sure

that you know how to use it; if there is no telephone, ask for the name of a neighbour whom you can call on in an emergency. There are several telephone numbers that you should write down; it is very unlikely that you will need to call anybody, but you must know where to ring if necessary. You will need the telephone number of the place the parents are going to, the doctor's telephone number, and the number of a neighbour or another adult you could call on. If there is a fire or other emergency you can always ring 999 and get the fire brigade, ambulance or police. A knowledge of First Aid is always advisable.

Make sure you know exactly what food to give to the child if he is hungry, whether you have to bath him or give him any medicines and at what time you should put him to bed.

Your responsibilities are solely towards the child in the absence of his parents who have placed this trust in you; you must never leave him in the house alone or go out of the room while he is in the bath. Remember also that you are in someone else's house and that you should not, therefore, eat any of their food or turn on any of their equipment (such as the television set) unless they have given you permission to do so.

Common Ailments and Infectious Diseases

The healthy child is bright, cheerful and active. When a child is ill he becomes peevish, sulky and tends to be miserable. He fails to take an interest in toys and games which usually amuse him. If he feels hot and his face is flushed, take his temperature. The normal temperature is about 37·0° (98·6°F) but a slight variation either above or below this may be normal. A figure up to 37·5°C (99·4°F) is usually considered normal. With children it is best to take the temperature by putting the thermometer in the armpit and holding the arm gently to the child's side. The temperature can be taken in the mouth, but it is unwise to do this with a young child in case he bites the thermometer and swallows the mercury in it. Nurses often take a temperature in a baby by putting the thermometer into the rectum.

If the temperature is above normal, the child should be put to bed.

Other signs of illness may be shown if he is pale, cold or listless. Sometimes he may be vomiting or have diarrhoea and he may complain of headache or pain in the stomach. If any of these signs are present, it is best to put the child to bed, or at least encourage him to rest, and call in a doctor. A temperature of 39°C or above would be another reason for seeking medical aid.

Some Common Ailments

Colds. The signs of a cold are fever, sometimes a slight sore throat, stuffiness and then a runny nose. A child with a cold should not be allowed to play with other children until he gets well and he may need to go to bed. His nose should be kept dry with a clean handkerchief or a soft tissue.

Constipation. A child usually has one soft motion a day, but it does not matter if the bowels are not open for one day or even more provided the motions are soft and passed without pain. If the opening of the bowels is delayed and the motions are hard, then a child's diet can be changed to include more fruit and vegetables and more fluids. Purgatives should be avoided if possible.

Diarrhoea. This is the frequent passing of a loose,

watery motion and is often associated with pains in the belly. If it is mild, it is best treated by restricting the child's diet to milk or milk and water. If the diarrhoea is severe, a doctor should be called in.

Infectious diseases

Germs, too small to be seen by the naked eye, are found everywhere; some are harmless, some produce or carry diseases. Infectious and contagious diseases are caused by germs which enter the body through the mouth with food or water, by being breathed into the lungs, through broken skin, or by transmission from the mother to the unborn baby.

Infectious diseases are spread by individuals and by objects. They are carried by air and dust, by infected food, water and milk, by flies and rats, or by infected articles such as bed linen, toys and books or by people carrying the disease. If you are exposed to germs which can cause a disease, this does not mean that you will necessarily catch it. In fact, often only a few of the people exposed to infection may get the illness. This is because they have developed immunity. The body, can be helped to resist infection by good nutrition, by drugs and immunization.

Immunity

Immunity is the power of resistance of the body against disease and especially against germs or their poisonous products (toxins). The body has many ways of protecting itself, one of which is that when you recover from an infectious disease you usually possess an immunity to it; this means that the body has formed certain substances (antibodies) which will, in future, prevent the germ of that disease from doing any harm. This is an 'acquired or active immunity'. It may be temporary or last a lifetime. Few people contract chicken-pox, whooping-cough or mumps more than once, because the immunity seems to last throughout life.

Immunity may be obtained by various other methods. A new born baby derives temporary immunity to certain diseases from his mother, provided she has had the disease. For this reason young babies seldom have measles or chicken-pox during the first few months of their life. This is an 'inherited immunity'.

Sometimes people have a very slight attack of an infectious disease which may pass almost unnoticed, but which produces antibodies which will protect them against any further attacks of the same disease.

Immunity may also be given by vaccination and immunization.

Vaccination. Vaccination is an almost sure and complete protection against smallpox. It is given when a person is going to travel into an area where there is smallpox or when he has recently been exposed to the infection. Vaccine is put on the arm and a little scratch is made, so that the germ in the live vaccine can enter the skin. A small sore spot results, which heals quite quickly and usually causes little upset. The germ in the vaccine comes from a very mild form of smallpox which

causes cowpox. The word vaccine is also used for other weakened germs and substances used for immunization.

Immunization. If weakened germs are given to a person he will contract only a very mild illness but will develop antibodies to protect him against a severe form of that disease in the future. This kind of immunization lasts for many years. In the same way an altered toxin can be injected to provoke the production of antibodies; diptheria is one of the diseases which can be prevented by this type of immunization.

Other diseases against which children can be protected in this way are whooping cough (Pertussis) and tetanus, which today are usually given with immunization against diptheria in a single injection called 'triple vaccine'. Three injections of this vaccine are given during the first year followed by a booster dose of combined diphtheria and tetanus vaccine at 5 years.

Poliomyelitis vaccine is given by mouth in three doses during the first year.

Measles vaccine is given once at about 15 months of age and protection against tuberculosis by B.C.G. at the beginning of the teens. German Measles can cause abnormal babies if a woman gets the illness during her pregnancy. It is, therefore, wise for all young girls to have a vaccination against German Measles and this is now done between 11 and 13 years of age.

The immunization usually given to babies is set out in the accompanying table.

Age	Immunization
4 to 6 months	Diphtheria/Tetanus/Pertussis vaccine Poliomyelitis vaccine (oral)
6 to 8 months	Diphtheria/Tetanus/Pertussis vaccine Poliomyelitis vaccine (oral)
12 to 14 months	Diphtheria/Tetanus/Pertussis vaccine Poliomyelitis vaccine (oral)
15 months	Measles vaccine
5 years or at school entry	Diphtheria/Tetanus vaccine Poliomyelitis vaccine (oral)
10 to 13 years	B.C.G.
11 to 13 years—girls	Rubella (German measles)
School leavers	Poliomyelitis vaccine Tetanus vaccine

Some infectious diseases

There is an interval between the time the person is exposed to an infectious disease and the time he experiences the first symptoms. This is called the incubation period. After this comes the active period of the disease with the symptoms and signs which are associated with it, followed by the period of recovery and convalescence. The incubation period and length of illness varies with each disease.

Measles

The incubation period is about 10–14 days at the end of which the patient appears to have a cold, with a runny nose and a slight cough, red eyes and a temperature. This lasts for about 4 days, after which, a red rash appears behind the ears and then covers the face and body. The rash fades slowly during the following week.

Whooping Cough (Pertussis)

The onset of this disease is gradual.

The incubation period is about 6–18 days; after this the patient appears to have a severe cold in the head and sometimes bronchitis for about a week. During this time the cough becomes more severe, especially at night. At this time 'the paroxysmal stage' begins to develop; the child makes 20 or 30 very short coughs and then draws in his breath making a characteristic whooping noise. Sometimes he vomits after coughing. The whooping stage lasts two weeks or longer, the whoops gradually becoming less frequent; after this the child gradually gets well though often a slight cough persists for some time. The only really good method of prevention is immunization.

Mumps

This disease has one of the longest incubation periods, about 17–21 days; there is a fairly sudden onset with swelling appearing at the back of the jaw on one or both sides. There is usually a certain amount of pain in the jaw and loss of appetite. After a few days the swellings which are really swollen glands, get smaller and recover their normal size.

Influenza

This disease comes on suddenly. The incubation period is 1–3 days. There is a high fever, shivering, pain in the back and limbs and headache. With some kinds of influenza there is a sore throat and a cough or a cold. If there are no complications the symptoms disappear after 4 or 5 days. There are vaccines which can be given against some types of influenza, but because of new strains of virus vaccines have to be changed fairly frequently.

Chicken pox

This is usually a mild disease in children. The incubation period is 11–21 days, usually about 18, after which small red spots appear on the child's chest and abdomen. The spots become little blisters and then scabs.

Rubella (German Measles)

The incubation period is between 14 and 21 days. It is a mild illness with a slight fever at the onset and some enlargement of glands, typically those around the neck. There is a rash of fine pink spots, which lasts only a few days. It is dangerous for women to contract rubella in the first 3 months of pregnancy because the virus may damage the unborn child; it is for this reason we try to see that women produce German Measles antibodies whilst they are still in their teens; either they are deliberately brought into contact with people who have the disease and thus get over it at an early age or they are given a vaccine to produce the antibodies.

Tonsillitis and Scarlet Fever

Sore throat is a common condition, but the most serious type causes painful red tonsils with a fever. The incubation period of tonsillitis is 1 to 3 days. The germ can spread to the middle ear causing ear ache and sometimes produces a toxin which causes scarlet fever. A scarlet rash, covering the whole body, appears one day after the start of the illness. As the rash fades, the skin peels.

Junior infant and child care syllabus

Session 1. The expectant mother. Birth of a baby. Local facilities for maternity care, including Child Health Clinics. Work of the Health Visitor. The Baby's room; heating, ventilation and lighting. Planning a room, with furniture and decoration.

Session 2. Preparing for Baby: the Baby's clothes – washing clothes. Choice of nappies. Perambulator, pushchair, carrying sling.

Session 3. The new-born baby: its appearance and needs. Stools and urine. Nappies – putting on, changing and washing.

Session 4. Caring for baby; mothering, sleep, activity, bathing.

Session 5. Feeding baby. Breast and bottle feeding; types of milk. Vitamins.

Session 6. Preparation of bottle feeds. Care of bottles and teats. Food poisoning.

Session 7. Weaning. Principles of nutrition. Diet up to 1 year. Planning and preparation of meals.

Session 8. One year's progress – normal physical and mental growth. Learning by imitation. Teeth. Sleep. Social Development and Activity.

Session 9. Care of the young child 1–2 years old. Feeding, clothing, exercise.

Session 10. Revision.

Junior infant and child care proficiency syllabus

Session 1. Revision of preparation for baby; room, clothes and equipment. Revision of care of the new-born baby, bathing and mothering.

Session 2. Revision of progress and care of the young child up to 2 years. Development up to the age of 5: play, toys and games. Story telling. Music.

Session 3. Physical care and hygiene of child up to 5 years. Washing. Care of Teeth. Bladder and bowels. Revision of changing nappies; Washing baby's clothes and nappies.

Session 4. Problems of children; fears, naughtiness, temper tantrums, jealousy. Feeding difficulties. Revision of feeding baby and making up feeds.

Session 5. Safety first and accidents. Treatment of burns and scalds. Demonstration of dangers in the home. Responsibilities when left in charge of children.

Session 6. Signs of illness. Common ailments. Taking temperature of child. Simple care for colds, constipation, diarrhoea. Diet and importance of fluids.

Session 7. Infectious diseases, immunity and immunization. Signs and symptoms of common infectious diseases. Revision.

Index

Index

Printed by John Blackburn Ltd., Leeds, England.